SCHOLAS

GRADES
4-6

Solve & Match
Math Practice
PAGES

50+ Motivating, Self-Checking Activities That
Help Kids Review and Master Essential Math Skills

ERIC CHARLESWORTH

New York • Toronto • London • Auckland • Sydney **Teaching** *Resources*
Mexico City • New Delhi • Hong Kong • Buenos Aires

This book is dedicated to Henry, who can count to 15 on a good day. And to Oscar, who may be able to prove the quadratic equation, for all we know. We'll find out once he starts talking.

—EC

Edited by Sarah Longhi
Cover design by Jason Robinson
Interior design by Melinda Belter

ISBN: 978-0-545-28816-3

1 2 3 4 5 6 7 8 9 10   40   18 17 16 15 14 13 12 11

CONTENTS

*Second level is more challenging than the first.

INTRODUCTION

If you've been looking for easy new ways to motivate your students to build and practice important math skills, this book of 50+ reproducible pages is for you.

Sure, students can benefit from practicing skills on their own. But independent practice often provides little support, leaving students who are unsure of their skills without guidance and even reinforcing bad habits when students repeat mistakes. The Solve & Match format was designed to overcome these pitfalls of independent work.

While students are solving the problems on these practice pages, they will be able to verify each answer by finding a matching answer on the page. If answers are not matching up, then students will quickly discover where their mistakes may be—and fix them on the spot. And when answers are matching up, students experience the satisfaction of knowing they are *getting it*!

When I began using the Solve & Match format for homework, the payoffs were clear from the beginning. Students began to:

• catch and fix their own mistakes

• stop skipping problems

• report that this type of homework was fun and ask for more!

The activities in this book have been aligned to the Common Core State Standards, and the contents are divided into easy-to-navigate sections. The reproducible format clearly lends itself well to homework assignments but can also be used for class warm-ups, morning work, or fun practice for fast finishers.

Some other features of interest in this book include the following:

Bonus challenge problems Each page features a "Triple Match Challenge," which offers students a more difficult problem to solve. The answer to this problem will match up with two other answers on the page, so students can check their work.

Word problems Several pages provide problem-solving practice with words. Students get to take their new skills to the basketball court, the kitchen, and the mall, and where they will face authentic story problems.

I hope these activities provide new options for the review and practice of essential math skills. And I hope your students not only enjoy the Solve & Match format but gain confidence as they take charge of their learning and sharpen their skills!

Name _____   Date _____

Adding Whole Numbers

Draw a line to match each sum on the left with one on the right.

LEFT	**RIGHT**
1. 67 + 85 =	**A.** 80 + 65 =
2. 43 + 199 =	**B.** 92 + 89 =
3. 29 + 80 =	**C.** 77 + 32 =
4. 56 + 56 =	**D.** 50 + 56 =
5. 79 + 102 =	**E.** 164 + 78 =
6. 84 + 77 =	**F.** 28 + 133 =
7. 129 + 16 =	**G.** 66 + 46 =
8. 57 + 49 =	**H.** 103 + 49 =

TRIPLE MATCH Challenge

What is the sum of 25, 37, 48, and 51? _____

Circle the answers that match above.

Name _____   Date _____

Subtracting Whole Numbers

Draw a line to match each difference on the left with one on the right.

LEFT	**RIGHT**
1. $260 - 112 =$	**A.** $300 - 153 =$
2. $384 - 295 =$	**B.** $296 - 148 =$
3. $181 - 42 =$	**C.** $176 - 31 =$
4. $256 - 111 =$	**D.** $140 - 81 =$
5. $524 - 377 =$	**E.** $240 - 81 =$
6. $78 - 19 =$	**F.** $160 - 45 =$
7. $200 - 41 =$	**G.** $258 - 169 =$
8. $250 - 135 =$	**H.** $234 - 95 =$

TRIPLE MATCH Challenge

Solve for x when $x + 132 = 277$. $x =$ _____

Circle the answers that match above.

Name _____   Date _____

Multiplying Whole Numbers

Draw a line to match each product on the left with one on the right.

LEFT   **RIGHT**

1. $23 \times 50 =$ **A.** $98 \times 10 =$

2. $49 \times 21 =$ **B.** $18 \times 22 =$

3. $38 \times 38 =$ **C.** $7 \times 147 =$

4. $39 \times 15 =$ **D.** $46 \times 25 =$

5. $102 \times 17 =$ **E.** $13 \times 45 =$

6. $36 \times 11 =$ **F.** $76 \times 19 =$

7. $72 \times 17 =$ **G.** $51 \times 34 =$

8. $20 \times 49 =$ **H.** $34 \times 36 =$

TRIPLE MATCH Challenge

Sam's Super Mart received a delivery of 51 boxes. Each box had 24 candy bars inside. In total, how many candy bars were included in the delivery? _____

Circle the answers that match above.

Name _____   Date _____

Dividing Whole Numbers

Draw a line to match each quotient on the left with one on the right.

LEFT	**RIGHT**
1. $56 \div 8 =$	**A.** $27 \div 3 =$
2. $64 \div 8 =$	**B.** $36 \div 12 =$
3. $42 \div 7 =$	**C.** $72 \div 9 =$
4. $25 \div 5 =$	**D.** $28 \div 4 =$
5. $63 \div 7 =$	**E.** $36 \div 6 =$
6. $20 \div 5 =$	**F.** $40 \div 8 =$
7. $27 \div 9 =$	**G.** $40 \div 10 =$
8. $24 \div 12 =$	**H.** $14 \div 7 =$

TRIPLE MATCH Challenge

One mystery number when multiplied by itself equals 81. What is the mystery number? _____

Circle the answers that match above.

Name _____   Date _____

Dividing Whole Numbers: 2 Digits

Draw a line to match each quotient on the left with one on the right.

LEFT   **RIGHT**

1. $247 \div 13 =$ **A.** $520 \div 40 =$

2. $615 \div 41 =$ **B.** $324 \div 18 =$

3. $198 \div 18 =$ **C.** $242 \div 11 =$

4. $754 \div 58 =$ **D.** $672 \div 56 =$

5. $396 \div 22 =$ **E.** $399 \div 19 =$

6. $294 \div 14 =$ **F.** $475 \div 25 =$

7. $720 \div 60 =$ **G.** $255 \div 17 =$

8. $374 \div 17 =$ **H.** $187 \div 17 =$

TRIPLE MATCH Challenge

Hope Elementary School has a total of 11 classrooms with the same number of students in each class. If there are 242 students in the school, how many are in each class? _____

Circle the answers that match above.

Name _____   Date _____

Mixed Whole-Number Operations I

Draw a line to match each answer on the left with one on the right.

LEFT

1. $30 \times 12 =$

2. $257 + 140 =$

3. $700 - 521 =$

4. $42 \times 14 =$

5. $365 \div 5 =$

6. $400 \times 3 =$

7. $756 - 633 =$

8. $291 + 41 =$

RIGHT

A. $200 - 127 =$

B. $614 + 586 =$

C. $369 \div 3 =$

D. $149 + 248 =$

E. $720 \div 2 =$

F. $45 + 134 =$

G. $147 \times 4 =$

H. $490 - 158 =$

TRIPLE MATCH Challenge

Solve this multistep problem: $12 \times 15 \times 2 = ?$

Circle the answers that match above.

Name _____   Date _____

Mixed Whole-Number Operations II

Solve each problem. Draw a line to match each answer on the left with one on the right.

LEFT	RIGHT
1. $24 \times 18 =$	**A.** $792 \div 11 =$
2. $1{,}296 - 1{,}157 =$	**B.** $200 - 119 =$
3. $39 \times 10 =$	**C.** $260 \div 2 \times 3 =$
4. $972 \div 12 =$	**D.** $54 \times 8 =$
5. $56 \times 3 \times 4 =$	**E.** $42 \times 16 =$
6. $59 + 322 =$	**F.** $522 - 141 =$
7. $36 \times 14 =$	**G.** $419 - 280 =$
8. $159 - 67 - 20 =$	**H.** $345 + 159 =$

TRIPLE MATCH Challenge

Solve this multistep problem: $(40 + 87) \times 3 = ?$

Circle the answers that match above.

Name _____   Date _____

Solving Word Problems: First Day of School

Draw a line to match each answer on the left with one on the right.
(NOTE: Only the numbers have to match.)

LEFT

1. Daniel figured out he attends school for 8 hours per day and the school year is 180 days long. If Daniel has perfect attendance, how many hours will he be in school this year?

_____

2. Ms. Carreras, the school secretary, ordered 25 boxes of pencils. Each box holds 40 pencils. How many pencils did she order in all?

_____

3. The P.E. teacher counted 43 tennis balls, 12 baseballs, and 4 footballs. How many balls were there in all?

_____

4. Last year the school had 432 students but this year they had 40 fewer students. How many students are at the school this year?

_____

RIGHT

A. Last year on the first day of school, 373 of the 432 students were on time and the rest were late. How many were late? _____

B. The art teacher, Mr. Pitch, bought 2 huge packages of paint brushes. Each package had 196 brushes. How many brushes did he have in total?

_____

C. In the cafeteria there were 500 spoons, 250 knives, and 250 forks. How many utensils were there in all?

_____

D. In sixth grade, the math students were asked to figure out how many minutes were in a day. Tara was the first one to come up with the right number. What was her answer?

_____

Solve & Match Math Practice Pages: Grades 4–6 © 2011 Eric Charlesworth, Scholastic Teaching Resources

Name _____   Date _____

Finding Patterns

Draw a line to match each value for ? on the left with one on the right.

LEFT

RIGHT

1. 45, ?, 55, 60, 65   ? = _____

A. 15, 30, 45, ?, 75   ? = _____

2. 12, 18, 24, ?, ___ ,   ? = _____

B. 22, ?, 66, 88, ___   ? = _____

3. 50, ?, ___ , 80, 90   ? = _____

C. 0, 25, ?, ___ , ___   ? = _____

4. ?, ___ , 64, 72, ___   ? = _____

D. 24, ___ , ?, 42, 48   ? = _____

5. 33, ?, ___ , ___ , 77   ? = _____

E. ___ , ___ , 24, 36, ?   ? = _____

TRIPLE MATCH Challenge

A number line began with the number 0 and had an interval of 20.
What was the third number after 0? _____

___   ___   ___   ___   ___   ___

Circle the answers that match above.

Name _____   Date _____

Finding the Range and Mode

For problems on the left, find the range. For problems on the right, find the mode. Draw a line to match each answer on the left with one on the right.

LEFT   **RIGHT**

1. 6, 9, 12, 14, 3   **A.** 36, 37, 37, 37, 36

Range = _____   Mode = _____

2. 20, 45, 5, 20, 42   **B.** 6, 0, 4, 6, 16

Range = _____   Mode = _____

3. 16, 50, 47, 13, 25   **C.** 5, 6, 8, 11, 11

Range = _____   Mode = _____

4. 8, 2, 5, 5, 7   **D.** 19, 19, 21, 23, 30

Range = _____   Mode = _____

5. 27, 9, 8, 20, 14   **E.** 24, 30, 40, 20, 40

Range = _____   Mode = _____

TRIPLE MATCH Challenge

Below is a list of the low temperatures in St. Paul, Minnesota, for a week in January. What is the range of temperatures? _____

-3°, -2°, 0°, -1°, 5°, 5°, 8°

Circle the answers that match above.

Solve & Match Math Practice Pages: Grades 4–6 © 2011 Eric Charlesworth, Scholastic Teaching Resources

Name _____ Date _____

Finding the Median

For each data set, find the median. Draw a line to match each answer on the left with one on the right.

LEFT

1. 14, 16, 19, 20, 22

Median = _____

2. 9, 10, 10, 13, 18

Median = _____

3. 27, 14, 12, 18, 20

Median = _____

4. 16, 19, 19, 14, 12

Median = _____

5. 12.2, 16, 19, 13, 4

Median = _____

RIGHT

A. 11, 12, 18, 19, 21

Median = _____

B. 34, 31, 0, 13, 7

Median = _____

C. 16, 16, 11, 24, 15

Median = _____

D. 16, 13, 10, 8, 5

Median = _____

E. 16, $16\frac{1}{2}$, 19, 19, 30

Median = _____

TRIPLE MATCH Challenge

Jarrell played in five basketball games. In the first game he didn't score. In the other four games he scored 8, 12, 10, and 19 points. What was his median score? _____

Circle the answers that match above.

Name _____   Date _____

Finding the Mean

For each data set, find the mean. Draw a line to match each answer on the left with one on the right.

LEFT	**RIGHT**
1. 12, 15, 18	**A.** 4, 7, 7
Mean = _____	Mean = _____
2. 3, 6, 10, 13	**B.** 8, 8, 8, 8
Mean = _____	Mean = _____
3. 5, 5, 5, 6, 9	**C.** 0, 10, 13, 17, 20
Mean = _____	Mean = _____
4. 1, 10, 10, 15, 20, 16	**D.** 11, 12, 13, 16, 16, 22
Mean = _____	Mean = _____

TRIPLE MATCH Challenge

Cindy played in three basketball games and averaged 12 points per game. If she scored 14 points in each of her first two games, how many points must she have scored in the third game? _____

Circle the answers that match above.

Solve & Match Math Practice Pages: Grades 4–6 © 2011 Eric Charlesworth, Scholastic Teaching Resources

Name _____   Date _____

Solving Word Problems: Sports Bash

Draw a line to match each answer on the left with one on the right.
(NOTE: Only the numbers have to match.)

LEFT

1. In their last seven games, the Lakers scored 127, 137, 107, 107, 113, 114, and 135 points. What was the range of their scores?

_____

2. Looking at the scores above, find the mode.

_____

3. Looking at the scores above, find the mean.

_____

4. Now find the median.

_____

RIGHT

A. In their last game, the Cowboys scored three touchdowns (six points each), kicked three extra points (one point each) and kicked three field goals (three points each). How many points did they score? _____

B. Tricia bowled three games and her scores were 98, 121, and 123. What was her average (mean) score?

_____

C. Over the course of six tennis matches, Genesis averaged 20 aces per match. How many aces did she have in total? _____

D. Doug swam 20 laps for four straight days and then swam 27 laps on the fifth day. How many laps did he swim in total? _____

Name _____   Date _____

Simplifying Fractions

Put each fraction into simplest form. Draw a line to match each answer on the left with one on the right.

LEFT

RIGHT

1. $\dfrac{6}{9}$ =

A. $\dfrac{10}{40}$ =

2. $\dfrac{10}{16}$ =

B. $\dfrac{4}{10}$ =

3. $\dfrac{8}{16}$ =

C. $\dfrac{40}{80}$ =

4. $\dfrac{10}{25}$ =

D. $\dfrac{15}{24}$ =

5. $\dfrac{3}{9}$ =

E. $\dfrac{8}{10}$ =

6. $\dfrac{12}{15}$ =

F. $\dfrac{8}{12}$ =

7. $\dfrac{10}{14}$ =

G. $\dfrac{9}{27}$ =

8. $\dfrac{2}{8}$ =

H. $\dfrac{15}{21}$ =

TRIPLE MATCH Challenge

In archery, Erick made 400 bull's-eyes out of 1,600 shots. Write the fraction of bull's-eyes in simplest form. _____

Circle the answers that match above.

Name _____   Date _____

Finding Fractional Parts of a Value

Draw a line to match each answer on the left with one on the right.

LEFT	**RIGHT**
1. Find $\frac{3}{5}$ of 50	**A.** Find $\frac{3}{4}$ of 80
2. Find $\frac{1}{2}$ of 72	**B.** Find $\frac{2}{3}$ of 45
3. Find $\frac{3}{4}$ of 20	**C.** Find $\frac{1}{2}$ of 80
4. Find $\frac{1}{4}$ of 100	**D.** Find $\frac{1}{3}$ of 30
5. Find $\frac{2}{5}$ of 100	**E.** Find $\frac{1}{3}$ of 54
6. Find $\frac{9}{10}$ of 20	**F.** Find $\frac{1}{4}$ of 100
7. Find $\frac{2}{3}$ of 90	**G.** Find $\frac{3}{5}$ of 60
8. Find $\frac{1}{5}$ of 50	**H.** Find $\frac{1}{4}$ of 60

TRIPLE MATCH Challenge

On Saturday, Pete's Pizza took 300 orders and $\frac{1}{10}$ of the people wanted mushroom pizzas. How many people wanted mushrooms? _____

Circle the answers that match above.

Name _____   Date _____

Adding & Subtracting Fractions

Draw a line to match each answer on the left with one on the right. Put each answer in simplest form.

LEFT   **RIGHT**

1. $\frac{3}{8} + \frac{2}{8} =$ A. $\frac{3}{12} + \frac{4}{12} =$

2. $\frac{4}{9} - \frac{1}{9} =$ B. $\frac{3}{9} + \frac{5}{9} =$

3. $\frac{2}{10} + \frac{3}{10} =$ C. $\frac{3}{10} + \frac{4}{10} =$

4. $\frac{11}{12} - \frac{4}{12} =$ D. $\frac{9}{10} - \frac{4}{10} =$

5. $\frac{5}{12} + \frac{3}{12} =$ E. $\frac{8}{9} - \frac{5}{9} =$

6. $\frac{9}{10} - \frac{2}{10} =$ F. $\frac{1}{8} + \frac{1}{8} =$

7. $\frac{2}{9} + \frac{6}{9} =$ G. $\frac{11}{12} - \frac{3}{12} =$

8. $\frac{4}{8} - \frac{2}{8} =$ H. $\frac{7}{8} - \frac{2}{8} =$

TRIPLE MATCH Challenge

Lacey was holding a cup of brown sugar when she tripped and spilled $\frac{3}{10}$ of a cup. How much sugar was left? _____

Circle the answers that match above.

Name _____   Date _____

Adding Fractions
With Unlike Denominators

Put each answer in simplest form. Draw a line to match each sum on the left with one on the right.

LEFT

1. $\frac{2}{3} + \frac{4}{5} =$

2. $\frac{1}{4} + \frac{3}{8} =$

3. $\frac{5}{7} + \frac{1}{2} =$

4. $\frac{1}{5} + \frac{2}{3} =$

5. $\frac{19}{20} + \frac{1}{2} =$

6. $\frac{2}{3} + \frac{11}{21} =$

7. $\frac{5}{8} + \frac{1}{4} =$

8. $\frac{4}{5} + \frac{1}{6} =$

RIGHT

A. $\frac{3}{10} + \frac{2}{3} =$

B. $\frac{7}{10} + \frac{3}{4} =$

C. $\frac{1}{8} + \frac{1}{2} =$

D. $\frac{3}{8} + \frac{1}{2} =$

E. $\frac{9}{14} + \frac{4}{7} =$

F. $\frac{8}{15} + \frac{1}{3} =$

G. $\frac{13}{15} + \frac{3}{5} =$

H. $\frac{6}{7} + \frac{1}{3} =$

TRIPLE MATCH Challenge

Emilio ran $\frac{3}{5}$ of a mile. After a water break, he ran another $\frac{3}{4}$ of a mile. Finally, he sprinted another $\frac{1}{10}$ of a mile. How many miles did he run in total? _____

Circle the answers that match above.

Name _____   Date _____

Adding & Subtracting Mixed Numbers

Put each answer in simplest form. Draw a line to match each answer on the left with one on the right.

LEFT	**RIGHT**
1. $2 + 3\frac{1}{2} =$	**A.** $4 - 1\frac{1}{4} =$
2. $4\frac{1}{2} - 3\frac{1}{4} =$	**B.** $1\frac{3}{4} + \frac{3}{4} =$
3. $2\frac{1}{3} + 1\frac{1}{2} =$	**C.** $7\frac{1}{2} - 2 =$
4. $6\frac{5}{6} - 3\frac{1}{3} =$	**D.** $1\frac{3}{4} - \frac{1}{2} =$
5. $1\frac{1}{4} + 1\frac{1}{2} =$	**E.** $3\frac{1}{5} + \frac{7}{10} =$
6. $4\frac{1}{3} - 2 =$	**F.** $1\frac{1}{6} + 1\frac{1}{6} =$
7. $2\frac{2}{5} + 1\frac{1}{2} =$	**G.** $1\frac{1}{6} + 2\frac{2}{3} =$
8. $3\frac{7}{10} - 1\frac{1}{5} =$	**H.** $5\frac{2}{3} - 2\frac{1}{6} =$

⌐TRIPLE MATCH Challenge ⌐

Complete this number pattern: $\frac{1}{4}$, $\frac{1}{2}$, $\frac{3}{4}$, 1, _____ .

Circle the answers that match above.

Name _____   Date _____

Multiplying Fractions

Put each answer in simplest form. Draw a line to match each product on the left with one on the right.

LEFT

1. $\frac{1}{2} \times \frac{4}{5} =$

2. $\frac{1}{8} \times \frac{4}{5} =$

3. $\frac{3}{5} \times \frac{3}{4} =$

4. $\frac{1}{8} \times \frac{2}{3} =$

5. $\frac{5}{6} \times \frac{4}{5} =$

6. $\frac{3}{8} \times \frac{1}{2} =$

7. $\frac{9}{10} \times \frac{1}{3} =$

8. $\frac{7}{8} \times \frac{2}{5} =$

RIGHT

A. $\frac{1}{2} \times \frac{3}{5} =$

B. $\frac{1}{4} \times \frac{7}{5} =$

C. $\frac{9}{10} \times \frac{1}{2} =$

D. $\frac{2}{3} \times \frac{3}{5} =$

E. $\frac{1}{5} \times \frac{1}{2} =$

F. $\frac{1}{4} \times \frac{1}{3} =$

G. $\frac{5}{3} \times \frac{2}{5} =$

H. $\frac{1}{4} \times \frac{3}{4} =$

TRIPLE MATCH Challenge

Felicia had a $\frac{1}{2}$-gallon bottle of fruit punch. She gave $\frac{3}{5}$ of her drink to her friend Jason. What fraction of a gallon did she give to Jason?

_____

Circle the answers that match above.

Name _____   Date _____

Multiplying Mixed Numbers

Put your answers in simplest form. Draw a line to match each product on the left with one on the right.

LEFT

RIGHT

1. $3\frac{1}{2} \times 2 =$

A. $6 \times 1\frac{1}{6} =$

2. $4\frac{1}{3} \times 1\frac{1}{2} =$

B. $3 \times 2\frac{1}{6} =$

3. $\frac{3}{5} \times 1\frac{2}{3} =$

C. $3\frac{1}{2} \times 3\frac{1}{3} =$

4. $3 \times 1\frac{1}{4} =$

D. $\frac{1}{4} \times 4 =$

5. $5\frac{3}{5} \times 2\frac{2}{3} =$

E. $1\frac{1}{2} \times 2\frac{1}{2} =$

6. $4\frac{1}{6} \times 3 =$

F. $2\frac{4}{5} \times 5\frac{1}{3} =$

7. $1\frac{1}{3} \times 1\frac{1}{2} =$

G. $25 \times \frac{1}{2} =$

8. $7 \times 1\frac{2}{3} =$

H. $\frac{3}{5} \times 3\frac{1}{3} =$

TRIPLE MATCH Challenge

Charlotte the Chef bought five packages of pastry. Each package weighed $2\frac{1}{3}$ pounds. How many pounds of pastry did she purchase in total? _____

Circle the answers that match above.

Name _____   Date _____

Dividing Fractions

Put your answers in simplest form. Draw a line to match each quotient on the left with one on the right.

LEFT

RIGHT

1. $\frac{1}{4} \div \frac{1}{8} =$

A. $\frac{2}{5} \div \frac{1}{6} =$

2. $\frac{5}{6} \div \frac{1}{2} =$

B. $\frac{3}{5} \div \frac{3}{4} =$

3. $\frac{1}{3} \div \frac{2}{5} =$

C. $\frac{3}{10} \div \frac{1}{4} =$

4. $\frac{4}{9} \div \frac{1}{3} =$

D. $\frac{1}{3} \div \frac{1}{6} =$

5. $\frac{4}{5} \div \frac{1}{3} =$

E. $\frac{5}{12} \div \frac{1}{4} =$

6. $\frac{2}{5} \div \frac{1}{2} =$

F. $\frac{8}{9} \div \frac{2}{3} =$

7. $\frac{2}{3} \div \frac{1}{5} =$

G. $\frac{1}{3} \div \frac{1}{10} =$

8. $\frac{9}{10} \div \frac{3}{4} =$

H. $\frac{2}{3} \div \frac{4}{5} =$

TRIPLE MATCH Challenge

At Silver Lake Pizza, it takes $2\frac{2}{3}$ containers of cheese for each large pizza. If a small pizza is half the size of a large pizza, how much cheese does it take to make a small pizza? _____

Circle the answers that match above.

Name _____   Date _____

Dividing Mixed Numbers

Put your answers in simplest form. Draw a line to match each quotient on the left with one on the right.

LEFT

1. $6 \div 1\frac{1}{2} =$

2. $5\frac{1}{2} \div \frac{1}{2} =$

3. $2 \div 3\frac{1}{2} =$

4. $1\frac{1}{4} \div 2 =$

5. $5 \div 2\frac{2}{3} =$

6. $6\frac{1}{2} \div 3 =$

7. $2\frac{1}{3} \div 3\frac{1}{2} =$

8. $1\frac{2}{3} \div 3 =$

RIGHT

A. $1 \div 1\frac{3}{4} =$

B. $2\frac{3}{4} \div \frac{1}{4} =$

C. $3 \div \frac{3}{4} =$

D. $3\frac{3}{4} \div 6 =$

E. $4\frac{2}{3} \div 7 =$

F. $3\frac{1}{4} \div 1\frac{1}{2} =$

G. $2\frac{1}{2} \div 1\frac{1}{3} =$

H. $\frac{5}{6} \div 1\frac{1}{2} =$

TRIPLE MATCH Challenge

Four people in a group are dividing up two and a half feet of ribbon equally. How much ribbon does each person receive? _____

Circle the answers that match above.

Name _____   Date _____

Mixed Fraction Practice

Put your answers in simplest form. Draw a line to match each answer on the left with one on the right.

LEFT

1. $1\frac{1}{3} + 1\frac{2}{3} =$

2. $\frac{4}{5} \times \frac{1}{2} =$

3. $\frac{7}{8} - \frac{1}{5} =$

4. $\frac{3}{8} \div \frac{1}{4} =$

5. $\frac{4}{9} - \frac{1}{3} =$

6. $1\frac{5}{8} + \frac{3}{4} =$

7. $\frac{7}{8} \times 1\frac{1}{2} =$

8. $\frac{4}{5} \div \frac{1}{3} =$

RIGHT

A. $4\frac{1}{2} \div 1\frac{1}{2} =$

B. $3\frac{1}{2} - 1\frac{1}{8} =$

C. $\frac{7}{8} + \frac{7}{16} =$

D. $\frac{2}{5} \div \frac{1}{6} =$

E. $\frac{9}{10} \times \frac{3}{4} =$

F. $\frac{7}{9} - \frac{2}{3} =$

G. $\frac{3}{4} \times 2 =$

H. $\frac{1}{5} + \frac{1}{5} =$

TRIPLE MATCH Challenge

Try to solve this multistep fraction problem:

$$\left(\frac{1}{2} + \frac{3}{8} \right) \times \left(\frac{4}{5} + \frac{7}{10} \right) = ? \ _____$$

Circle the answers that match above.

Name _____ Date _____

Solving Word Problems: Now We're Cookin'

Draw a line to match each answer on the left with one on the right.
(NOTE: Only the numbers have to match.)

LEFT

RIGHT

1. Lauren is using spices for her cake recipe. First she uses $\frac{2}{3}$ tablespoon of cinnamon. Later she adds $\frac{1}{6}$ tablespoon more. What fraction of a tablespoon did she use in all? _____

A. Matt is making smoothies in his blender. The recipe calls for $\frac{1}{3}$ cup of milk and $\frac{1}{2}$ cup of water. How much total liquid goes into the recipe? _____

2. The cake is supposed to cook for $\frac{1}{3}$ of one hour. How many minutes is that? _____

B. Matt has 32 ounces of frozen blueberries. But he only uses $\frac{1}{4}$ of them for his recipe. How many ounces does he use? _____

3. When she put it in the oven, it was 2 centimeters high. When it was finished baking, it had risen $2\frac{1}{2}$ times as high. How many centimeters high was it then? _____

C. Matt ended up making $2\frac{1}{2}$ pitchers of his smoothie. If each pitcher makes 8 servings, how many servings does he make? _____

4. She cut the cake in half. Then she cut each half into quarters. How many pieces of cake did she have? _____

D. Matt loved his recipe. He drank $1\frac{1}{2}$ cups at breakfast, 1 cup at lunch and $2\frac{1}{2}$ cups at dinner. How many cups did he drink in all? _____

Name _____   Date _____

Converting Fractions to Decimals

Convert each fraction to a decimal value. Draw a line to match each answer on the left with one on the right.

LEFT

RIGHT

1. $\frac{4}{10}$ =

2. $\frac{2}{20}$ =

3. $\frac{3}{5}$ =

4. $\frac{4}{5}$ =

5. $\frac{13}{20}$ =

6. $\frac{35}{50}$ =

7. $\frac{9}{10}$ =

8. $\frac{1}{2}$ =

A. $\frac{65}{100}$ =

B. $\frac{1}{10}$ =

C. $\frac{50}{100}$ =

D. $\frac{2}{5}$ =

E. $\frac{16}{20}$ =

F. $\frac{90}{100}$ =

G. $\frac{12}{20}$ =

H. $\frac{14}{20}$ =

TRIPLE MATCH Challenge

Find the sum of $\frac{3}{10}$ and $\frac{3}{5}$. Then convert your answer into a decimal. _____

Circle the answers that match above.

Name _____   Date _____

Adding Decimals

Draw a line to match each sum on the left with one on the right.

LEFT

1. 3.6 + 2.2 =

2. 5.71 + 4.5 =

3. 3.98 + 1.1 =

4. 4 + 2.34 =

5. 5.1 + 7.77 =

6. 6.81 + 2.41 =

7. 3.9 + 4.12 =

8. 4.65 + 1.7 =

RIGHT

A. 2.9 + 5.12 =

B. 7.2 + 5.67 =

C. 2.34 + 3.46 =

D. 3.44 + 2.9 =

E. 5.21 + 5 =

F. 2 + 7.22 =

G. 1.91 + 3.17 =

H. 3.3 + 3.05 =

TRIPLE MATCH Challenge

Steven was using two types of sand for a science project. One kind weighed 2.72 pounds and the other kind weighed 5.3 pounds. How much sand did he have in total? _____

Circle the answers that match above.

Name _____   Date _____

Subtracting Decimals

Draw a line to match each difference on the left with one on the right.

LEFT   **RIGHT**

1. $7.84 - 1.19 =$ **A.** $5.1 - 2.78 =$

2. $2.65 - 0.32 =$ **B.** $5.6 - 1.4 =$

3. $5.98 - 1.17 =$ **C.** $6.21 - 1.4 =$

4. $3.56 - 2.3 =$ **D.** $5.56 - 4.3 =$

5. $4.77 - 1.8 =$ **E.** $8.17 - 5.2 =$

6. $6.03 - 1.77 =$ **F.** $8.85 - 2.2 =$

7. $3.9 - 1.58 =$ **G.** $4 - 1.67 =$

8. $8 - 3.8 =$ **H.** $8.52 - 4.26 =$

TRIPLE MATCH Challenge

Juan went to the store and bought a pack of basketball cards that cost $1.19. He also bought a carton of orange juice for $4.55. If he paid with a ten-dollar bill, how much change did he receive? _____

Circle the answers that match above.

Name _____   Date _____

Multiplying Decimals

Draw a line to match each product on the left with one on the right.

LEFT

1. $2.2 \times 3.3 =$

2. $4 \times 2.5 =$

3. $2.4 \times 1.2 =$

4. $8 \times 3.5 =$

5. $5.8 \times 1.1 =$

6. $4.5 \times 3 =$

7. $6.25 \times 6 =$

8. $1.6 \times 1.4 =$

RIGHT

A. $2.9 \times 2.2 =$

B. $0.5 \times 20 =$

C. $25 \times 1.5 =$

D. $16 \times 0.14 =$

E. $3.63 \times 2 =$

F. $4.8 \times 0.6 =$

G. $16 \times 1.75 =$

H. $9 \times 1.5 =$

TRIPLE MATCH Challenge

Elizabeth found out that one of her favorite collectible buttons was worth $1.21. She sold six of them for that price to another collector. How much money did she make? _____

Circle the answers that match above.

Dividing Decimals

Name _____   Date _____

Draw a line to match each quotient on the left with one on the right.

LEFT	RIGHT
1. $8 \div 0.2 =$	**A.** $7.2 \div 2.4 =$
2. $42 \div 2.5 =$	**B.** $8.4 \div 8 =$
3. $9 \div 0.03 =$	**C.** $16 \div 0.4 =$
4. $4.4 \div 2.2 =$	**D.** $27 \div 0.09 =$
5. $3.6 \div 1.2 =$	**E.** $4 \div 2.5 =$
6. $4.2 \div 4 =$	**F.** $12 \div 0.4 =$
7. $7.2 \div 0.24 =$	**G.** $8.4 \div 0.5 =$
8. $9.6 \div 6 =$	**H.** $3 \div 1.5 =$

TRIPLE MATCH Challenge

Boxes of markers cost $1.50 each. If Ms. Furman has $45, how many boxes can she buy for her class? _____

Circle the answers that match above.

Name _____   Date _____

Mixed Decimal Practice

Draw a line to match each answer on the left with one on the right.

LEFT	**RIGHT**
1. $3.4 + 2.3 =$	**A.** $0.3 \times 5 =$
2. $6.1 - 3.05 =$	**B.** $2 \times 1.2 =$
3. $8 \times 0.3 =$	**C.** $3.22 + 3.93 =$
4. $1.44 \div 1.2 =$	**D.** $3.9 - 2.7 =$
5. $12.3 \div 8.2 =$	**E.** $3 - 0.07 =$
6. $17.6 - 10.45 =$	**F.** $1.9 \times 3 =$
7. $4 \times 3.5 =$	**G.** $2.8 \div 0.2 =$
8. $1.6 + 1.33 =$	**H.** $2.45 + 0.6 =$

TRIPLE MATCH **Challenge**

Try to solve this multistep problem: $(0.35 + 0.25) \times 4 = ?$ _____

Circle the answers that match above.

Name _____   Date _____

Mixed Fraction and Decimal Practice 1

Draw a line to match each fraction on the left with an equivalent decimal on the right.

LEFT

1. $\frac{1}{2} + \frac{3}{4} =$

2. $\frac{5}{8} + \frac{1}{8} =$

3. $\frac{4}{5} - \frac{1}{10} =$

4. $1\frac{1}{3} - \frac{5}{6} =$

5. $\frac{2}{5} \times 2 =$

6. $2\frac{3}{4} \times 1 =$

7. $3 \div 1\frac{1}{3} =$

8. $9 \div 1\frac{1}{2} =$

RIGHT

A. $1.85 - 0.6 =$

B. $0.25 \times 3 =$

C. $3.75 \times 0.6 =$

D. $0.34 + 0.16 =$

E. $3.2 + 2.8 =$

F. $2 - 1.2 =$

G. $5.5 \div 2 =$

H. $1.4 \div 2 =$

TRIPLE MATCH Challenge

Jen bought potatoes priced at \$3.75 per pound. If she purchased $\frac{1}{3}$ of a pound, how much did Jen spend? _____

Circle the answers that match above.

Name _____   Date _____

Mixed Fraction and Decimal Practice II

Draw a line to match each fraction on the left with an equivalent decimal on the right.

LEFT	**RIGHT**
1. $\frac{4}{5} + \frac{2}{5} =$	**A.** $6 \times 2.5 =$
2. $\frac{5}{8} + \frac{1}{2} =$	**B.** $0.9 \div 0.8 =$
3. $2 - \frac{3}{4} =$	**C.** $5.25 \div 1.5 =$
4. $\frac{3}{4} - \frac{1}{5} =$	**D.** $1.8 \div 0.3 =$
5. $\frac{1}{3} \times 18 =$	**E.** $0.5 \times 0.5 =$
6. $\frac{1}{2} \times \frac{1}{2} =$	**F.** $1.5 - 0.3 =$
7. $5 \div \frac{1}{3} =$	**G.** $0.75 - 0.2 =$
8. $3\frac{1}{2} \div 1 =$	**H.** $1.05 + 0.2 =$

TRIPLE MATCH Challenge

Try to solve this multistep problem: $(4.3 + 2.7) \times \frac{1}{2} = ?$ _____

Circle the answers that match above.

Name _____   Date _____

Solving Word Problems: Ice Cream Truck

Solve each word problem. Draw a line to match each answer on the left with one on the right. (NOTE: Only the numbers have to match.)

LEFT

RIGHT

1. Chris drives an ice cream truck around the neighborhood. Today he drove for $2\frac{3}{4}$ hours. How many minutes did he drive? _____

2. He sold six bomb pops for $1.35 each. How much money did he get for the bomb pops? _____

3. One customer bought three ice cream cones that cost $1.30 each. If the customer paid with a $5 bill, how much change did she receive?

_____

4. Each time he drives around the block, Chris drives $\frac{1}{5}$ of a mile. How many times does he need to drive around the block to go 3 miles?

_____

A. Chris's cousin Andrei bought $16.20 worth of ice cream. But Chris gave it to him for half price. How much did he charge Andrei? _____

B. Chris bought packages of spoons that cost $2.50 each. If he spent a total of $37.50, how many packages did he buy? _____

C. Chris's last customer gave him a tip. He gave three quarters, three dimes, and a nickel. How big a tip was it?

_____

D. At the end of the day Chris counted up 33 five-dollar bills. How much money is that? _____

Name _____ Date _____

Converting Fractions to Percentages

Convert each fraction to a percentage value. Draw a line to match each answer on the left with one on the right.

LEFT

1. $\frac{2}{5}$ =

2. $\frac{1}{10}$ =

3. $\frac{7}{10}$ =

4. $\frac{12}{25}$ =

5. $\frac{20}{25}$ =

6. $\frac{3}{4}$ =

7. $\frac{3}{5}$ =

8. $\frac{25}{50}$ =

RIGHT

A. $\frac{24}{50}$ =

B. $\frac{4}{10}$ =

C. $\frac{6}{10}$ =

D. $\frac{1}{2}$ =

E. $\frac{5}{50}$ =

F. $\frac{75}{100}$ =

G. $\frac{4}{5}$ =

H. $\frac{14}{20}$ =

TRIPLE MATCH Challenge

William was able to complete 16 of 20 passes in his football game. What was his completion percentage? _____

Circle the answers that match above.

Name _____   Date _____

Finding Percentages of a Value

Draw a line to match each answer on the left with one on the right.

LEFT

1. 50% of 16 =

2. 10% of 20 =

3. 30% of 40 =

4. 90% of 20 =

5. 50% of 18 =

6. 25% of 100 =

7. 40% of 50 =

8. 10% of 70 =

RIGHT

A. 80% of 25 =

B. 50% of 36 =

C. 20% of 10 =

D. 50% of 50 =

E. 40% of 30 =

F. 40% of 20 =

G. 20% of 45 =

H. 100% of 7 =

_TRIPLE MATCH **Challenge**

What is 6% of 200? _____

Circle the answers that match above.

Name _____   Date _____

Solving Word Problems: Mall Madness

Draw a line to match each answer on the left with one on the right.
(NOTE: Only the numbers have to match.)

LEFT

1. Felicia had a 30%-off coupon to use at the mall. If she used the coupon on a $20 shirt, how much did she save?

_____

2. She also had a 10%-off coupon for the movies. She used the coupon for four tickets. The regular price of the tickets was $6 each. With the coupon, how much did she spend? _____

3. However, she didn't like the movie and only stayed to watch 50% of it. If the movie was 102 minutes long, how many minutes did she stay? _____

4. She left the mall at 8:22 and got home at 9:07. How long did it take her to get home? _____

RIGHT

A. Milton went to the mall and bought three soccer balls that cost $17 each. How much did he spend in total?

_____

B. He played a game at the arcade where he took 8 basketball shots and made 75% of them. How many shots did he make? _____

C. He bought a pair of shin guards. He paid with $30 and received $8.40 in change. How much did the shin guards cost? _____

D. The mall has 135 stores, and amazingly, Milton went in one-third of them. How many stores did he explore? _____

Name _____   Date _____

Finding Perimeters

Find the perimeter of each polygon. Draw a line to match each answer on the left with one on the right.

LEFT

1. Square

Perimeter = _____

9 cm

9 cm

2. Triangle

Perimeter = _____

8 cm   9 cm

10 cm

3. Rectangle

Perimeter = _____

6 cm

5 cm

4. Rhombus

Perimeter = _____

5 cm   5 cm

5. Regular Pentagon

Perimeter = _____

5 cm   5 cm

RIGHT

A. Irregular Quadrangle

Perimeter = _____

8 cm
9 cm
5 cm
3 cm

B. Rectangle

Perimeter = _____

6 cm
4 cm

C. Triangle

Perimeter = _____

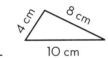
4 cm   8 cm
10 cm

D. Parallelogram

Perimeter = _____

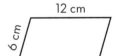
12 cm
6 cm

E. Triangle

Perimeter = _____

10.5 cm   10.5 cm
6 cm

TRIPLE MATCH Challenge

One side of a regular hexagon is 6 centimeters. What is the perimeter of the hexagon? _____

Circle the answers that match above.

Name _____ Date _____

Finding Triangle Angles

In each triangle, find the missing angle. Draw a line to match each answer on the left with one on the right.

LEFT

RIGHT

1. 70° 45° ? = ____

A. 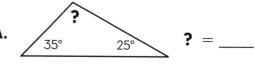 35° 25° ? = ____

2. 30° 30° ? = ____

B. 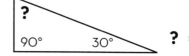 100° 38° ? = ____

3. 65° 73° ? = ____

C. 71° 44° ? = ____

4. 100° 40° ? = ____

D. ? 90° 30° ? = ____

5. 60° 60° ? = ____

E. 58° 82° ? = ____

─ TRIPLE MATCH **Challenge** ─

An isosceles triangle has one angle that measures 96 degrees. What is the measure of each of the other two angles? _____

Circle the answers that match above.

Name _____   Date _____

Finding Quadrilateral Angles

In each polygon, find the missing angle. Draw a line to match each answer on the left with one on the right.

LEFT   **RIGHT**

1. [rectangle with right angles and ?] _____   A. [75° 100° / 105° ?] _____

2. [100° ? / 80° 100°] _____   B. [? 48° / 70° 130°] _____

3. [65° 70° / 120° ?] _____   C. [112° 94° / 64° ?] _____

4. [68° ? / 112° 68°] _____   D. [85° 85° / 85° ?] _____

5. [108° ? / 72° 72°] _____   E. [? 80° / 80° 92°] _____

TRIPLE MATCH Challenge

A parallelogram has two angles that are 75 degrees. What is the measure of each of the other two angles? _____

Circle the answers that match above.

Name _____   Date _____

Finding the Area of Rectangles

Find the area of each rectangle. Draw a line to match each answer on the left with one on the right.

LEFT   **RIGHT**

1.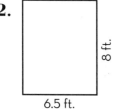

8 ft.

9 ft.

Area = _____

A.

16 ft.

5 ft.

Area = _____

2.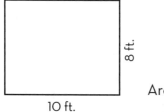

8 ft.

6.5 ft.

Area = _____

B.

12 ft.

6 ft.

Area = _____

3.

8 ft.

10 ft.

Area = _____

C.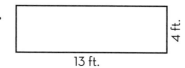

13 ft.

4 ft.

Area = _____

4.

20 ft.

4.5 ft.

Area = _____

D.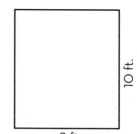

10 ft.

9 ft.

Area = _____

TRIPLE MATCH Challenge

When a rectangle is bisected, it creates two squares that each have four sides of 6 centimeters. What is the area of the rectangle? _____

Circle the answers that match above.

Name _____   Date _____

Finding the Area of Triangles

Find the area of each triangle. Draw a line to match each answer on the left with one on the right.

LEFT   **RIGHT**

1. Area = _____ 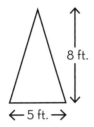   **A.** Area = _____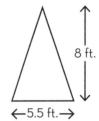

2. Area = _____   **B.** Area = _____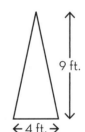

3. Area = _____   **C.** Area = _____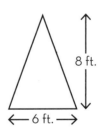

4. Area = _____   **D.** Area = _____

TRIPLE MATCH **Challenge**

Find the area of a triangle with a base of 5 feet and a height of 7.2 feet. _____

Circle the answers that match above.

Solve & Match Math Practice Pages: Grades 4–6 © 2011 Eric Charlesworth, Scholastic Teaching Resources

Name _____   Date _____

Finding the Area of Trapezoids and Parallelograms

Find the area of each quadrilateral. Draw a line to match each answer on the left with one on the right.

LEFT   **RIGHT**

1. Area = _____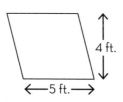

A. Area = _____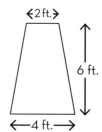

2. Area = _____

B. Area = _____

3. Area = _____

C. Area = _____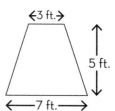

4. Area = _____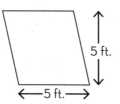

D. Area = _____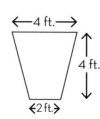

TRIPLE MATCH Challenge

A parallelogram has a height of 6 feet and an area of 72 square feet. What is the measurement of the base? _____

Circle the answers that match above.

Solve & Match Math Practice Pages: Grades 4–6 © 2011 Eric Charlesworth, Scholastic Teaching Resources

Name _____   Date _____

Finding the Volume of Rectangular Prisms

Find the volume of each rectangular prism. Draw a line to match each answer on the left with one on the right.

LEFT   **RIGHT**

1. 6 cm, 6 cm, 6 cm   Volume = _____

A. 6 cm, 4 cm, 4 cm   Volume = _____

2. 3 cm, 8 cm, 4 cm   Volume = _____

B. 6 cm, 5 cm, 4 cm   Volume = _____

3. 5 cm, 6 cm, 8 cm   Volume = _____

C. 2 cm, 9 cm, 12 cm   Volume = _____

4. 3 cm, 4 cm, 10 cm   Volume = _____

D. 5 cm, 4 cm, 12 cm   Volume = _____

TRIPLE MATCH **Challenge**

A set of 12 identical cubes have sides of 2 centimeters. What is the total volume of all the cubes? _____

Circle the answers that match above.

Name _____ Date _____

Solving One-Step Equations I

Solve for x. Draw a line to match each answer on the left with one on the right.

LEFT

RIGHT

1. $x + 3 = 10$ x = _____

A. $4x = 36$ x = _____

2. $x - 3 = 10$ x = _____

B. $x + 20 = 26$ x = _____

3. $4x = 32$ x = _____

C. $x + 11 = 24$ x = _____

4. $6x = 18$ x = _____

D. $x - 6 = 2$ x = _____

5. $x - 10 = 12$ x = _____

E. $9x = 27$ x = _____

6. $x + 5 = 14$ x = _____

F. $9x = 36$ x = _____

7. $2x = 8$ x = _____

G. $x + 8 = 30$ x = _____

8. $8x = 48$ x = _____

H. $2x = 14$ x = _____

TRIPLE MATCH Challenge

Boat rides in Myriad Harbor cost $2. A group arrived and paid $18 for everyone to go on the boat. How many people were in the group? _____

Circle the answers that match above.

Solve & Match Math Practice Pages: Grades 4–6 © 2011 Eric Charlesworth, Scholastic Teaching Resources

Name _____   Date _____

Solving One-Step Equations II

Solve for x. Draw a line to match each answer on the left with one on the right.

LEFT

RIGHT

1. $17x = 136$ x = _____

A. $5x = 75$ x = _____

2. $12x = 288$ x = _____

B. $x + 4 = 67$ x = _____

3. $x - 51 = 11$ x = _____

C. $13x = 104$ x = _____

4. $x - 36 = 27$ x = _____

D. $x + 82 = 100$ x = _____

5. $x + 48 = 100$ x = _____

E. $37 - x = 13$ x = _____

6. $x + 37 = 81$ x = _____

F. $2x = 104$ x = _____

7. $21x = 378$ x = _____

G. $x + 135 = 197$ x = _____

8. $14x = 210$ x = _____

H. $3x = 132$ x = _____

TRIPLE MATCH Challenge

Solve for x if $\frac{x}{2} = 12$. x = _____

Circle the answers that match above.

Name _____   Date _____

Solving Two-Step Equations

Solve for x. Draw a line to match each answer on the left with one on the right.

LEFT   **RIGHT**

1. $3x - 6 = 24$ $x =$ _____   **A.** $10x - 50 = 50$ $x =$ _____

2. $2x + 9 = 33$ $x =$ _____   **B.** $9x + 14 = 77$ $x =$ _____

3. $5x - 7 = 13$ $x =$ _____   **C.** $2x - 1 = 3$ $x =$ _____

4. $10x + 18 = 38$ $x =$ _____   **D.** $3x - 24 = 0$ $x =$ _____

5. $4x - 5 = 23$ $x =$ _____   **E.** $11x + 20 = 119$ $x =$ _____

6. $5x - 4 = 41$ $x =$ _____   **F.** $7x + 12 = 40$ $x =$ _____

7. $4x + 10 = 30$ $x =$ _____   **G.** $3x + 5 = 41$ $x =$ _____

8. $9x + 8 = 80$ $x =$ _____   **H.** $8x - 10 = 30$ $x =$ _____

TRIPLE MATCH Challenge

Greg's brother Pete is three years more than twice as old as him. The sum of their ages is 30. How old is Greg? _____

Circle the answers that match above.

Name _____   Date _____

Evaluating Expressions

In each expression, find the value when x = 3 and y = 5. Draw a line to match each answer on the left with one on the right.

LEFT   **RIGHT**

1. $x + 7 =$ **A.** $4y - 8 =$

2. $2x + 8 =$ **B.** $5y - 24 =$

3. $x + 20 =$ **C.** $6y - 6 =$

4. $3x - 4 =$ **D.** $4y =$

5. $10x - 6 =$ **E.** $y + 18 =$

6. $5x + 5 =$ **F.** $y =$

7. $4x =$ **G.** $2y =$

8. $x - 2 =$ **H.** $3y - 1 =$

TRIPLE MATCH Challenge

If x = 3 and y = 5, then what is $3x - 9 + 1y$? _____

Circle the answers that match above.

Name _____   Date _____

Solving Word Problems: Guess My Age!

Draw a line to match each answer on the left with one on the right.
(NOTE: Only the numbers have to match.)

LEFT

1. Gisella is four years older than Maria. The sum of their ages is 22. How old is Gisella? _____

2. Henry is six years younger than Beckett. The sum of their ages is 30. How old is Beckett? _____

3. The difference between Carl's and John's ages is five years. The sum of their ages is 27. If Carl is older than John, how old is he? _____

4. Sarah is one-quarter the age of her grandmother. If her grandmother is 45 years older than she is, how old is Sarah? _____

RIGHT

A. Ollie is three times the age of his dog and his dog is two years older than his cat. If Ollie's cat is four years old, how old is Ollie? _____

B. Elaine is one year older than Jerry and the product of their ages is 42. What is the sum of their ages?

_____

C. Walker is three times the age of Hunter. If the sum of the two boys' ages is 20, how old is Walker?

_____

D. If he were one year older, Jimmy would be exactly half the age of his 34-year-old Aunt Tina. How old is Jimmy? _____

Name _____   Date _____

Mixed Practice I

Solve each problem. Draw a line to match each answer on the left with one on the right.

LEFT

1. $2\frac{1}{2} \times 4 =$

2.

   18 cm   21 cm

   24 cm

   Perimeter = _____

3. What is 24% of 50?

4. $4.9 - 1.3 =$

5. $40 \times 5 =$

6. $72 \div 8 =$

RIGHT

A. What is x if $x + 19 = 29$? $x =$ ____

B. $1.8 \times 2 =$

C. What is the range of 4, 8, 10, 12 and 16?

D. What is the mode of 8, 10, 9, 7.5 and 9?

E. $9 \times 7 =$

F. Complete the pattern: 140, 160, 180, ____

TRIPLE MATCH Challenge

If $x = 1.5$ and $y = 2$, what is $(6x + 6y) \times 3$? _____

Circle the answers that match above.

Name _____ Date _____

Mixed Practice II

Solve each problem. Draw a line to match each answer on the left with one on the right.

LEFT   **RIGHT**

1. $47 \times 3 =$ **A.** $2.56 + 1.44 =$

2. $154 + 302 =$ **B.** $24 \times 2\frac{2}{3} =$

3.   **C.**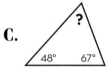

    Volume = _____   ? = _____

4. What is the mean of 1, 4, 5, 5 and 5?   **D.** $114 \times 4 =$

5. $\frac{1}{4} + 1\frac{3}{4} =$ **E.** $210 - 69 =$

6. $13 \times 5 =$ **F.** $0.7 \div 0.35 =$

TRIPLE MATCH Challenge

Corliss is one year older than his brother Charles and twice as old as his sister Camilla. If Camilla is 13 years old, what is the sum of the three ages? _____

Circle the answers that match above.

Name _____   Date _____

Mixed Practice III

Draw a line to match each answer on the left with one on the right.

LEFT

RIGHT

1. $68 \times 5 =$

A. $4.2 \div 0.2 =$

2. $2\frac{3}{4} \div \frac{1}{4} =$

B. $29 \times 3 =$

3.

┌──────────────┐
│   │ 8 cm
└──────────────┘
    20 cm

Area = _____

C. 9.5   10   10.5   ?   11.5

? = _____

4. $13.87 + 7.13 =$

D. $20.84 - 8.24 =$

5. $1{,}131 \div 13 =$

E. What is $\frac{4}{5}$ of 200?

6. $4.2 \times 3 =$

F. $680 \div 2 =$

TRIPLE MATCH Challenge

Five squares have side lengths of 1, 2, 3, 4, and 5 inches. What is the mean value of the square areas? _____

Circle the answers that match above.

Name _____   Date _____

Mixed Practice IV

Draw a line to match each answer on the left with one on the right.

LEFT   **RIGHT**

1. $149 + 361 =$ **A.** $64 \times 0.5 =$

2. $32 \times \frac{3}{8} =$ **B.** $480 \div 10 \div 2 =$

3. Solve for x if $3x - 22 = 74$ **C.** Solve for x if $20x - 45 = 215$

    x = _____   x = _____

4. What is 96% of 25?   **D.** $1{,}530 \div 3 =$

5. $3.25 \times 4 =$ **E.** $\frac{5}{8} + 2\frac{1}{2} =$

6. $\frac{5}{16} \div \frac{1}{10} =$ **F.** Find the mean of 8, 13, 13, and 14

    _____

TRIPLE MATCH Challenge

A freight truck is carrying an unknown number of boxes. Each box in the truck contains 200 MP3 players. If there are a total of 6,400 MP3 players on the box, how many boxes are on the truck? _____

Circle the answers that match above.

Answer Key

PAGE 5
1. 152
2. 242
3. 109
4. 112
5. 181
6. 161
7. 145
8. 106
A. 145
B. 181
C. 109
D. 106
E. 242
F. 161
G. 112
H. 152
TMC: 161

PAGE 6
1. 148
2. 89
3. 139
4. 145
5. 147
6. 59
7. 159
8. 115
A. 147
B. 148
C. 145
D. 59
E. 159
F. 115
G. 89
H. 139
TMC: 145

PAGE 7
1. 1,150
2. 1,029
3. 1,444
4. 585
5. 1,734
6. 396
7. 1,224
8. 980
A. 980
B. 396
C. 1,029

D. 1,150
E. 585
F. 1,444
G. 1,734
H. 1,224
TMC: 1,224

PAGE 8
1. 7
2. 8
3. 6
4. 5
5. 9
6. 4
7. 3
8. 2
A. 9
B. 3
C. 8
D. 7
E. 6
F. 5
G. 4
H. 2
TMC: 9

PAGE 9
1. 19
2. 15
3. 11
4. 13
5. 18
6. 21
7. 12
8. 22
A. 13
B. 18
C. 22
D. 12
E. 21
F. 19
G. 15
H. 11
TMC: 22 students

PAGE 10
1. 360
2. 397
3. 179
4. 588
5. 73
6. 1,200
7. 123
8. 332
A. 73
B. 1,200
C. 123
D. 397
E. 360
F. 179
G. 588
H. 332
TMC: 360

PAGE 11
1. 432
2. 139
3. 390
4. 81
5. 672
6. 381
7. 504
8. 72
A. 72
B. 81
C. 390
D. 432
E. 672
F. 381
G. 139
H. 504
TMC: 381

PAGE 12
1. 1,440
2. 1,000
3. 59
4. 392
A. 59
B. 392
C. 1,000
D. 1,440

PAGE 13
1. 50
2. 36
3. 60
4. 48
5. 44
A. 60
B. 44
C. 50
D. 36
E. 48
TMC: 60

PAGE 14
1. 11
2. 40
3. 37
4. 6
5. 19
A. 37
B. 6
C. 11
D. 19
E. 40
TMC: 11

PAGE 15
1. 19
2. 10
3. 18
4. 16
5. 13
A. 18
B. 13
C. 16
D. 10
E. 19
TMC: 10

PAGE 16
1. 15
2. 8
3. 6
4. 12
A. 6
B. 8
C. 12
D. 15
TMC: 8

PAGE 17
1. 30
2. 107
3. 120
4. 114
A. 30
B. 114
C. 120
D. 107

PAGE 18
1. $\frac{2}{3}$
2. $\frac{5}{8}$
3. $\frac{1}{2}$
4. $\frac{2}{5}$
5. $\frac{1}{3}$
6. $\frac{4}{5}$
7. $\frac{5}{7}$
8. $\frac{1}{4}$
A. $\frac{1}{4}$
B. $\frac{2}{5}$
C. $\frac{1}{2}$
D. $\frac{5}{8}$
E. $\frac{4}{5}$
F. $\frac{2}{3}$
G. $\frac{1}{3}$
H. $\frac{5}{7}$
TMC: $\frac{1}{4}$

PAGE 19
1. 30
2. 36
3. 15
4. 25
5. 40
6. 18
7. 60
8. 10
A. 60
B. 30
C. 40
D. 10
E. 18
F. 25
G. 36
H. 15
TMC: 30

PAGE 20
1. $\frac{5}{8}$
2. $\frac{1}{3}$
3. $\frac{1}{2}$
4. $\frac{7}{12}$
5. $\frac{2}{3}$
6. $\frac{7}{10}$
7. $\frac{8}{9}$
8. $\frac{1}{4}$
A. $\frac{7}{12}$
B. $\frac{8}{9}$
C. $\frac{7}{10}$
D. $\frac{1}{2}$
E. $\frac{1}{3}$
F. $\frac{1}{4}$
G. $\frac{2}{3}$
H. $\frac{5}{8}$
TMC: $\frac{7}{10}$ cup

PAGE 21
1. $1\frac{7}{15}$
2. $\frac{5}{8}$
3. $1\frac{3}{14}$
4. $\frac{13}{15}$
5. $1\frac{9}{20}$
6. $1\frac{4}{21}$
7. $\frac{7}{8}$
8. $\frac{29}{30}$
A. $\frac{29}{30}$
B. $1\frac{9}{20}$
C. $\frac{5}{8}$
D. $\frac{7}{8}$
E. $1\frac{3}{14}$
F. $\frac{13}{15}$
G. $1\frac{7}{15}$
H. $1\frac{4}{21}$
TMC: $1\frac{9}{20}$

PAGE 22
1. $5\frac{1}{2}$
2. $1\frac{1}{4}$
3. $3\frac{5}{6}$
4. $3\frac{1}{2}$
5. $2\frac{3}{4}$
6. $2\frac{1}{3}$
7. $3\frac{9}{10}$
8. $2\frac{1}{2}$
A. $2\frac{3}{4}$
B. $2\frac{1}{2}$
C. $5\frac{1}{2}$
D. $1\frac{1}{4}$

E. 3 $\frac{9}{10}$
F. 2 $\frac{1}{3}$
G. 3 $\frac{5}{6}$
H. 3 $\frac{1}{2}$
TMC: 1 $\frac{1}{4}$

PAGE 23
1. $\frac{2}{5}$
2. $\frac{1}{10}$
3. $\frac{9}{20}$
4. $\frac{1}{12}$
5. $\frac{2}{3}$
6. $\frac{3}{16}$
7. $\frac{3}{10}$
8. $\frac{7}{20}$
A. $\frac{3}{10}$
B. $\frac{7}{20}$
C. $\frac{9}{20}$
D. $\frac{2}{5}$
E. $\frac{1}{10}$
F. $\frac{1}{12}$
G. $\frac{2}{3}$
H. $\frac{3}{16}$
TMC: $\frac{3}{10}$

PAGE 24
1. 7
2. 6 $\frac{1}{2}$
3. 1
4. 3 $\frac{3}{4}$
5. 14 $\frac{14}{15}$
6. 12 $\frac{1}{2}$
7. 2
8. 11 $\frac{2}{3}$
A. 7
B. 6 $\frac{1}{2}$
C. 11 $\frac{2}{3}$
D. 1
E. 3 $\frac{3}{4}$
F. 14 $\frac{14}{15}$
G. 12 $\frac{1}{2}$
H. 2
TMC: 11 $\frac{2}{3}$

PAGE 25
1. 2
2. 1 $\frac{2}{3}$
3. $\frac{5}{6}$
4. 1 $\frac{1}{3}$
5. 2 $\frac{2}{5}$
6. $\frac{4}{5}$
7. 3 $\frac{1}{3}$
8. 1 $\frac{1}{5}$
A. 2 $\frac{2}{5}$
B. $\frac{4}{5}$
C. 1 $\frac{1}{5}$
D. 2
E. 1 $\frac{2}{3}$
F. 1 $\frac{1}{3}$
G. 3 $\frac{1}{3}$
H. $\frac{5}{6}$
TMC: 1 $\frac{1}{3}$ containers

PAGE 26
1. 4
2. 11
3. $\frac{4}{7}$
4. $\frac{5}{8}$
5. 1 $\frac{7}{8}$
6. 2 $\frac{1}{6}$
7. $\frac{2}{3}$
8. $\frac{5}{9}$
A. $\frac{4}{7}$
B. 11
C. 4
D. $\frac{5}{8}$
E. $\frac{2}{3}$
F. 2 $\frac{1}{6}$
G. 1 $\frac{7}{8}$
H. $\frac{5}{9}$
TMC: $\frac{5}{8}$ foot

PAGE 27
1. 3
2. $\frac{2}{5}$
3. $\frac{27}{40}$
4. 1 $\frac{1}{2}$
5. $\frac{1}{9}$
6. 2 $\frac{3}{8}$
7. 1 $\frac{5}{16}$
8. 2 $\frac{2}{5}$
A. 3
B. 2 $\frac{3}{8}$
C. 1 $\frac{5}{16}$
D. 2 $\frac{2}{5}$
E. $\frac{27}{40}$
F. $\frac{1}{9}$
G. 1 $\frac{1}{2}$
H. $\frac{2}{5}$
TMC: 1 $\frac{5}{16}$

PAGE 28
1. $\frac{5}{6}$ tablespoon
2. 20
3. 5
4. 8
A. $\frac{5}{6}$ cup
B. 8
C. 20
D. 5

PAGE 29
1. 0.4
2. 0.1
3. 0.6
4. 0.8
5. 0.65
6. 0.7
7. 0.9
8. 0.5
A. 0.65
B. 0.1
C. 0.5
D. 0.4
E. 0.8
F. 0.9
G. 0.6
H. 0.7
TMC: 0.9

PAGE 30
1. 5.8
2. 10.21
3. 5.08
4. 6.34
5. 12.87
6. 9.22
7. 8.02
8. 6.35
A. 8.02
B. 12.87
C. 5.8
D. 6.34
E. 10.21
F. 9.22
G. 5.08
H. 6.35
TMC: 8.02 pounds

PAGE 31
1. 6.65
2. 2.33
3. 4.81
4. 1.26
5. 2.97
6. 4.26
7. 2.32
8. 4.2
A. 2.32
B. 4.2
C. 4.81
D. 1.26
E. 2.97
F. 6.65
G. 2.33
H. 4.26
TMC: $4.26

PAGE 32
1. 7.26
2. 10
3. 2.88
4. 28
5. 6.38
6. 13.5
7. 37.5
8. 2.24
A. 6.38
B. 10
C. 37.5
D. 2.24
E. 7.26
F. 2.88
G. 28
H. 13.5
TMC: $7.26

PAGE 33
1. 40
2. 16.8
3. 300
4. 2
5. 3
6. 1.05
7. 30
8. 1.6
A. 3
B. 1.05
C. 40
D. 300

E. 1.6
F. 30
G. 16.8
H. 2
TMC: 30

PAGE 34
1. 5.7
2. 3.05
3. 2.4
4. 1.2
5. 1.5
6. 7.15
7. 14
8. 2.93
A. 1.5
B. 2.4
C. 7.15
D. 1.2
E. 2.93
F. 5.7
G. 14
H. 3.05
TMC: 2.4

PAGE 35
1. 1¼ (1.25)
2. ¾ (0.75)
3. ⁷/₁₀ (0.7)
4. ½ (0.5)
5. ⅘ (0.8)
6. 2¾ (2.75)
7. 2¼ (2.25)
8. 6
A. 1.25 (1¼)
B. 0.75 (¾)
C. 2.25 (2¼)
D. 0.5 (½)
E. 6
F. 0.8 (4/5)
G. 2.75 (2¾)
H. 0.7 (⁷/₁₀)
TMC: $1.25

PAGE 36
1. 1⅕ (1.2)
2. 1⅛ (1.125)
3. 1¼ (1.25)
4. ¹¹/₂₀ (0.55)
5. 6
6. ¼ (0.25)

7. 15
8. 3½ (3.5)
A. 15
B. 1.125 (1⅛)
C. 3.5 (3½)
D. 6
E. 0.25 (¼)
F. 1.2 (1⅕)
G. 0.55 (¹¹/₂₀)
H. 1.25 (1¼)
TMC: 3½ (3.5)

PAGE 37
1. 165
2. $8.10
3. $1.10
4. 15
A. $8.10
B. 15
C. $1.10
D. 165 dollars

PAGE 38
1. 40%
2. 10%
3. 70%
4. 48%
5. 80%
6. 75%
7. 60%
8. 50%
A. 48%
B. 40%
C. 60%
D. 50%
E. 10%
F. 75%
G. 80%
H. 70%
TMC: 80%

PAGE 39
1. 8
2. 2
3. 12
4. 18
5. 9
6. 25
7. 20
8. 7
A. 20

B. 18
C. 2
D. 25
E. 12
F. 8
G. 9
H. 7
TMC: 12

PAGE 40
1. $6
2. $21.60
3. 51
4. 45 minutes
A. $51
B. 6
C. $21.60
D. 45

PAGE 41
1. 36 cm
2. 27 cm
3. 22 cm
4. 20 cm
5. 25 cm
A. 25 cm
B. 20 cm
C. 22 cm
D. 36 cm
E. 27 cm
TMC: 36 cm

PAGE 42
1. 65°
2. 120°
3. 42°
4. 40°
5. 60°
A. 120°
B. 42°
C. 65°
D. 60°
E. 40°
TMC: 42°

PAGE 43
1. 90°
2. 80°
3. 105°
4. 112°
5. 108°

A. 80°
B. 112°
C. 90°
D. 105°
E. 108°
TMC: 105°

PAGE 44
1. 72 sq. ft.
2. 52 sq. ft.
3. 80 sq. ft.
4. 90 sq. ft.
A. 80 sq. ft.
B. 72 sq. ft.
C. 52 sq. ft.
D. 90 sq. ft.
TMC: 72 sq. ft.

PAGE 45
1. 20 sq. ft.
2. 24 sq. ft.
3. 18 sq. ft.
4. 22 sq. ft.
A. 20 sq. ft.
B. 22 sq. ft.
C. 18 sq. ft.
D. 24 sq. ft.
TMC: 18 sq. ft.

PAGE 46
1. 12 sq. ft.
2. 20 sq. ft.
3. 18 sq. ft.
4. 25 sq. ft.
A. 20 sq. ft.
B. 18 sq. ft.
C. 25 sq. ft.
D. 12 sq. ft.
TMC: 12 ft.

PAGE 47
1. 216 cu. ft.
2. 96 cu. ft.
3. 240 cu. ft.
4. 120 cu. ft.
A. 96 cu. ft.
B. 120 cu. ft.
C. 216 cu. ft.
D. 240 cu. ft.
TMC: 96 cu. ft.

PAGE 48
1. 7
2. 13
3. 8
4. 3
5. 22
6. 9
7. 4
8. 6
A. 9
B. 6
C. 13
D. 8
E. 3
F. 4
G. 22
H. 7
TMC: 9

PAGE 49
1. 8
2. 24
3. 62
4. 63
5. 52
6. 44
7. 18
8. 15
A. 15
B. 63
C. 8
D. 18
E. 24
F. 52
G. 62
H. 44
TMC: 24

PAGE 50
1. 10
2. 12
3. 4
4. 2
5. 7
6. 9
7. 5
8. 8
A. 10
B. 7
C. 2
D. 8

E. 9
F. 4
G. 12
H. 5
TMC: 9 years old

PAGE 51
1. 10
2. 14
3. 23
4. 5
5. 24
6. 20
7. 12
8. 1
A. 12
B. 1
C. 24
D. 20
E. 23
F. 5
G. 10
H. 14
TMC: 5

PAGE 52
1. 13 years old
2. 18 years old
3. 16 years old
4. 15 years old
A. 18 years old
B. 13 years old
C. 15 years old
D. 16 years old

PAGE 53
1. 10
2. 63 cm
3. 12
4. 3.6
5. 200
6. 9
A. 10
B. 3.6
C. 12
D. 9
E. 63
F. 200
TMC: 63

PAGE 54
1. 141
2. 456
3. 64 cu. cm
4. 4
5. 2
6. 65
A. 4
B. 64
C. 65°
D. 456
E. 141
F. 2
TMC: 64

PAGE 55
1. 340
2. 11
3. 160 square units
4. 21
5. 87
6. 12.6
A. 21
B. 87
C. 11
D. 12.6
E. 160
F. 340
TMC: 11

PAGE 56
1. 510
2. 12
3. 32
4. 24
5. 13
6. 3⅛
A. 32
B. 24
C. 13
D. 510
E. 3⅛
F. 12
TMC: 32

Skill: _____

Draw a line to match each answer on the left with one on the right.

LEFT   **RIGHT**

1.   A.

2.   B.

3.   C.

4.   D.

5.   E.

6.   F.